Soar Like An Eagle

Reign Like A King

Rev. Seaton D. Wilson

Soar Like An Eagle, Reign Like A King
Copyright © 2010 by Seaton & Jean Wilson
P.O. Box 716, Christiansted, St. Croix, VI 00821
s2jcelove@yahoo.com
(340) 277-9094 • (340) 277-9201

All rights reserved. No part of this book should be reproduced, in any form, without the written permission from its publishers, except for short quotations in speeches, critical articles or reviews.

ISBN: 978-0-578-05960-0
Library of Congress Control Number: 2010909466

All quotations from the Bible, except those marked (KJV), are taken from the New International version, (R) copyright © 1973, 1978, 1984 by International Bible Society. Published by Zondervan, Grand Rapids, Michigan, 49530 U.S.A., All rights reserved.

Quotations marked (KJV) are taken from
the King James Version.

Editorial Development by
Minister Mary D. Edwards, Leaves of Gold Consulting, LLC
LeavesOfGoldConsulting.com

Book cover and page design by
Shannon Crowley, Treasure Image & Publishing
TreasureImagePublishing.com

Dedication

This book is dedicated first and foremost to the Lord Jesus Christ, as an instrument to transform the lives of Christians and contribute to spiritual revival worldwide. Thank you, Jesus, for this privilege.

It is also dedicated to Jean, the queen of my heart, who has shared my sorrow and joys, pain and pleasure, failure and success, in life and ministry for thirty-one years. She has also actively embraced my God-given vision to impact the world for Christ through preaching, teaching, writing, praying and whatever other means to fulfill this purpose. Thank you, Jean.

SOAR LIKE AN EAGLE ♛ REIGN LIKE A KING

Endorsements

It gives me great pleasure to endorse my dear husband's book, **Soar Like An Eagle, Reign Like A King**. I have been happily married for 31 years to this man of God. Recently, we renewed our marriage vows in Jamaica, our birthplace.

As a pastor's wife, it is difficult for me to find someone to share my deepest thoughts and challenges with. My husband always finds time to listen to me and give good advice. He is truly my best friend.

Not only is he a good friend, but he is a wise and loving father to our two sons, Joseph and Christoph. He is a praying man. As a result of us standing in prayer together, I was able to conceive a son after waiting for 11 years, and after the doctor said we couldn't have children.

Pastor Seaton D. Wilson is a man who knows his priorities and keeps them straight. He finds time for his family, his church and his community.

In all the years that I have known him he has been an avid reader and has studied constantly all kinds of books, especially books that are deep and difficult. The book that you are about to read is the result of a life of deep studies, thinking and experience. May the Holy Spirit use it to transform your life and make you soar into what God wants you to be.

REV. JEAN WILSON
WIFE AND CO-PARTNER IN MINISTRY

If you have been looking for a deeper and a more exciting walk with God, you have picked up the right book. Pastor Seaton Wilson has unlocked the treasures of heaven and has accumulated a wealth of biological, physiological and spiritual insight on this incredible creature called the eagle. This work is of high importance to the serious believer who wants to become more innovative and creative. When God uses a creature such as the eagle to illustrate a point, it is of utmost importance that we duly give that creature our undivided attention. This book gives us practical illustrations of this magnificent creature and shows us how to conquer the hopelessness and despairs of our present world situations.

You can influence your environment and control your circumstances again by gleaning from the pages of this outstanding work. Allow the information on the pages of this thesaurus of wisdom to shine on the pathway of your destiny. Pastor Wilson, thank you for taking the time to research and apply the life of an eagle to our lives.

DR. PEPE & ANGELA RAMNATH
RESEARCH SCIENTIST & SENIOR PASTORS
MIRAMAR CHRISTIAN CENTER, INTERNATIONAL – FLORIDA, USA

Soar like an Eagle, Reign like a King unlocks a treasure chest of amazing spiritual truths in the imagery of the Golden Eagle. You can count them, savor them, and give thanks to God for the spiritual wisdom and insights outlined in this book. You will discover blessings that can be used in your daily life, especially in difficult times; these truths can be applied for a lifetime.

Endorsements

Rev. Wilson uses illustrations and imagery that draws you closer to God's heart and lets you know that you can be a Golden Eagle Christian and weather the storms of life, no matter how fierce the wind may blow. Rev. Wilson mixes Biblical stories with the Golden Eagle's way of life in a batter of glorious truths that bake into a delightful spiritual dessert. In this book you will discover God's ability to strengthen us to overcome life's difficulties and struggles in every area of our lives. This is a must read book!

ARTHUR NEMBHARD, MDIV, DD
SENIOR PASTOR OF THE DESIRE OF ALL
NATIONS CHURCH, TAMPA, FLORIDA
& SENIOR CHAPLAIN, LIFE PATH HOSPICE

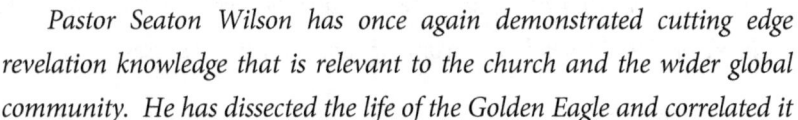

Pastor Seaton Wilson has once again demonstrated cutting edge revelation knowledge that is relevant to the church and the wider global community. He has dissected the life of the Golden Eagle and correlated it via similes to God and a mature Christian.

Reading this book will cause you to envision yourself soaring like the eagle, thus causing you to live on a higher Christian plain. Those who are sick of living a ground dove-like lifestyle, will begin to set their sights higher and soar out of their sickness and their low living.

Christians who are running away from the tricks and stratagems of the enemy will spend time to be developed in the word to defeat the enemy every time with the word of God.

This book, in my opinion, is a revelatory classic for our time and for the future generation.

I, therefore, enthusiastically concur with Pastor Wilson that we should develop our "nictitating membranes" and become double vision like the Golden Eagle; therefore, giving us the ability to see with inner eyes. In conclusion, I highly recommend this book to you and your friends.

PASTOR ORAL HAZELL, D.D.
SENIOR PASTOR GLOBAL LIFE CHURCH
ST. THOMAS, UNITED STATES VIRGIN ISLANDS

Seldom will you have the opportunity to read a book that answers the most pivotal question ever posed to man, 'Who are you?'

From Adam and Eve to the Sons of Sceva, the proper answer to this question has determined the success or failure of our actions. Finally we have an answer that fits, is scriptural, and (if believed), will unfold to the believer in Christ a whole new world of opportunity and success.

This book is a must read for intercessors, warriors, and watchmen. A source of deliverance, freedom and inspiration for all who read it.

REV. BARBARA A. WILLIAMS, PRESIDENT
THE MINISTRY OF THE WATCHMAN, INTERNATIONAL
CLEVELAND, OHIO & DETROIT, MICHIGAN

I cannot help but think that **Soar Like An Eagle, Reign Like A King** *apart from the Bible, should be one of the books every family should have, to help guide their sons and daughters into a wholesome life; one pleasing to God and man.*

Endorsements

Chapters 9-12 in this book have shown how we should conduct ourselves in courtship without violating ourselves until there is a marriage; how to wait for, and attract the right mate to ourselves. Many of us have lost the true essence of life, because we had forced our way, prematurely, into areas that would have been beautiful waiting to chart and discover.

I congratulate Seaton and Jean on this endeavor to make the secrets of good living known by the pattern set by the Golden Eagle. Both Seaton and Jean have lived an exemplary life of marriage, lasting 31 years and is still going strong. Their relationship to each other truly patterns the way of the Golden Eagle. They are both qualified to bring this good news to the world and, in so doing, will help to make those who will read and become aware of the tenets of this message to excel in their own lives as well.

Congratulations to those who will read and pattern **Soar Like An Eagle, Reign like A King.**

REGNA PAGE, B.SC, MSM
TRAINING SPECIALIST
PAGE-ONE FINISHING ACADEMY

God has given Pastor Wilson the ability to graphically illustrate how the female and male Golden Eagles go about courtship for marriage.

When you have the love of God in your life you can begin to follow the examples of Christ and build your relationship on the solid Rock, which is Christ Jesus. For those who are seeking a better understanding and desire wisdom in selecting a mate for marriage, like me, I find this book extremely profound.

The details that are described in the chapters dealing with courtship and testing by the female eagle are life changing. There is much to be learnt from the Golden Eagle and how each of us should proceed with cultivating a love relationship that may result in marriage. This has given me new insight on how to increase my expectations during courtship and to stand on my principles.

RAMELLE T. LEE
AUTHOR, <u>STEP INTO HIS GREATNESS</u>
DETROIT, MICHIGAN

Acknowledgements

I say thanks to Rev. Lloyd Allen for sharing with me his summary information on the Golden Eagle in 1998, which eventually lead to the writing of this book.

Thanks must go also to Ms. Riyyah Bat Moshe-McCoy, who tediously transcribed my two sermons, "Be An Eagle Christian," from tape to written form. It is from this that I developed this book.

Thanks also to Minister Mary Edwards, who so ably did the editing in a professional manner. I thank her also for encouragements and advice.

Special thanks to my wife, Jean, who did all the typing and most of the e-mail correspondences for this book.

Thanks to all my endorsers as listed in this book and all others who have helped in some way.

Thank You All.

TABLE OF CONTENTS

Dedication 3
Endorsements 5
Acknowledgements 11
Foreword 15
Introduction 17

CHAPTER ONE 19
Preliminary Comments and Proposition

CHAPTER TWO 23
The Golden Eagle Lives At High Altitude

CHAPTER THREE 31
The Golden Eagle Flies Faster Than Other Birds

CHAPTER FOUR 35
The Golden Eagle Has Brilliant Eyesight

CHAPTER FIVE 41
The Golden Eagle Feeds Mostly On Living Things

CHAPTER SIX 49
Four Enemies Of The Golden Eagle

CHAPTER SEVEN 57
Spiritual Truths We Should Learn From The Golden Eagle and Its Enemies

CHAPTER EIGHT 69
The Golden Eagle and Family Life: A Biblical Overview

CHAPTER NINE 77
The Golden Eagle and Family Life: COURTSHIP and MARRIAGE, Part 1

CHAPTER TEN.. 83
The Golden Eagle and Family Life: COURTSHIP and MARRIAGE, Part 2

CHAPTER ELEVEN 99
The Golden Eagle And Family Life: BUILDING A HOME

CHAPTER TWELVE.. 105
The Golden Eagle And Family Life: CHILD REARING

CHAPTER THIRTEEN 111
The Golden Eagle Is King Over Its Domain

Conclusion 115

About The Author 121

Booklets by Seaton D. Wilson 122

Foreword

Have you ever felt like you wanted to spread your spiritual wings and fly?

Well, you can. So, get ready to take off.

In his book, Soar Like An Eagle, Reign Like A King, Pastor Seaton D. Wilson tells us how.

This book uses examples from the life of the Golden Eagle to give profound revelatory insights into the Christian life. Analogies such as the eagle's ability to soar quickly, see with its eyes closed, conquer its enemies, reign like a king and much more are used.

Of course, once God's people make up their minds to soar, you can be sure there will be opposition to deal with. Wilson doesn't hesitate to talk straight to us about how to turn these barriers into stepping stones. I found this part of the book particularly helpful. Indeed, it was a revelation to me to learn that if the eagle is in its nest when it senses a storm or a hurricane coming, it goes to the edge of the rock, flies out into the storm, and uses the wind force of the storm to cause it to soar higher. Simply put, the eagle does not fly away from nor fight the storm; it uses it to its own advantage.

In a similar way, spiritually speaking, an eagle-like Christian uses the storms and hurricanes of life, which are the problems, trials and sufferings that he or she experiences, to soar to higher levels in Christ. He or she does not fight nor run from these negative experiences but capitalizes on them.

Friends, it's time for God's people to stop scratching around in the chicken coop and soar like an eagle. We must do this if we want to reign like a king and take hold of the rich inheritance that our Heavenly Father has promised to us. Yes, in perilous times like these, we need the revelatory teaching and strategies that Pastor Seaton D. Wilson shares in this powerful book. I encourage you to purchase a copy for yourself and one or more copies for a friend.

MINISTER MARY D. EDWARDS • DETROIT, MICHIGAN
FOUNDER, THE CALLED AND READY WRITERS
THECALLEDANDREADYWRITERS.ORG

LEAVES OF GOLD CONSULTING, LLC
LEAVESOFGOLDCONSULTING.COM

Introduction

This book, "*SOAR LIKE AN EAGLE, REIGN LIKE A KING*," began in seminal form in 1998. On a Saturday morning, at a "*United Ministers Meeting*," at First Assembly of God, 5 Newleigh Road, Mandeville, Jamaica. On that day, Rev. Lloyd Allen, pastor of Bethsaida church, distributed a three-page summary of the life of the Golden Eagle.

After I read it, I was fascinated by the new insights I gained. I wanted to preach on it right away, but was restrained by the Holy Spirit, I believe, because it was not yet the fullness of time to do so. However, in the year 2000, I felt the urgent desire to preach a two-part sermon on consecutive Sundays, entitled, "*Be an Eagle Christian,*" and I responded accordingly. The response was overwhelming. I got more requests for cassette tapes of these sermons than any other in my thirty years of preaching, up to that time. Since then, I have done extensive research on the Golden Eagle and other eagles. As a result, God has given me great insight in applying the eagle's life to the Christian's life. I have preached on the analogies of the Golden Eagle and the Christian life in the Caribbean, Canada, and the United States, for the past ten (10) years.

I had always wanted to transcribe these sermons from cassette tapes and publish them in book form, but it was not until 2009 that I made the decision to do so. I got them transcribed in January 2010 and then I carefully edited them into this book, assisted by my lovely wife, Jean.

My objective in writing this book is to educate, inspire and motivate Christians to experience a life of forward and upward mobility in Christ.

I invite you, therefore, to SOAR LIKE AN EAGLE AND REIGN LIKE A KING, as you read this book. Let us begin.

Chapter One

PRELIMINARY COMMENTS AND PROPOSITION

The Bible uses metaphors, similes and illustrations to teach about human and Christian life. For example, it uses sheep, goats, leopards, serpents, doves and eagles. The text, Isaiah 40:30-31, says, *"Even youths grow tired and weary, and young men stumble and fall; But those who hope in the Lord will renew their strength. They will soar on wings like eagles; they will run and not grow weary, they will walk and not be faint."*

This significant text uses the eagle as an illustration to teach, by implication, some very important truths about renewal, overcoming difficulties, victory and progress in the Christian life. Note carefully that the above passage says, *"Even youths grow tired and weary,"* (verse 30). These experiences are greater problems for older people. However, there is a solution to these problems of tiredness and weariness when we view them from a spiritual perspective. Psalm 103:5 re-enforces Isaiah 40:30-31.

There are two outstanding truths about the eagle that are illustrative of the Christian life that are clearly stated. However, there are other amazing truths we can learn from the eagle that are stated in other parts of the Bible and in extra-biblical sources that have been known through observation and scientific studies. The two remarkable things that are clearly mentioned in the text are as follows: How the eagle renews its strength and its intriguing ability to soar.

These subjects of renewal and soaring teach important lessons that both Christians and non-Christians can learn. There is a providential reason why God has caused me to present this message at this time, because it is extremely relevant in this hour of trials and testing in our society and the world at large. Further truths about the eagle will be gleaned from other scriptures and sources.

Chapter One

People are desperate today. Crimes of all kinds are on the increase in many parts of the world. More people are committing suicide, as a way of escape from trials, meaninglessness, purposelessness and emptiness in their lives. Even children and people who have wealth, fame and power are turning to alcohol, drugs and ending their lives.

I would like us to understand that whatever happens outside in the world happens in the church also. Everything that has ever happened in history outside the church has happened in the church. As a matter of fact, it happened amongst Jesus twelve disciples when Judas committed suicide. So, we shouldn't say it has not and will not happen in the church. There are people in church who would have committed suicide and other crimes but they have been afraid. People have told me, including people in the church, that they have contemplated taking their own lives. I wonder how many of you right now have thought about it, but you are afraid to do it. If we live like the eagle, we will overcome negative challenges and more, because we will renew our strength and soar in the realm of the Spirit. God says, *"He gives strength to the weary and increases the power of the weak. Even youth grow tired and weary and young men stumble and fall,"* but those who hope in the Lord are the ones who renew their strength like eagles. Those who have faith in Christ are the ones who are like eagles.

I propose to you that a Christian should live like an eagle. I will present some amazing characteristics of the Golden Eagle that illustrate spiritual truths that we should apply to our own lives.

Chapter Two

THE GOLDEN EAGLE LIVES AT HIGH ALTITUDE

First, the Golden Eagle lives at high altitude. It does not live on low plain. The eagle lives in mountains or spends most of its time on high mountain rocks. It seldom comes down to earth unless on special occasions. Likewise, God did not make man to live morally and spiritually low. He wants us to live in the high realms of the spirit. Even when we lower ourselves in humility to lift up others who are down, we should still stay in the high realms of the spirit. The eagle comes down specifically to acquire food and then returns to its high place. It also comes down to help other eagles that are going through molting seasons and to attack other birds and animals that are trespassing in its territory.

Ground Dove *Golden Eagle*

Some years ago I spoke on the comparison between eagles and ground doves. Ground doves do not live up high. They live low down. People who live sinful lives live at a low altitude morally and spiritually. They are like ground doves; focusing on earthly things. These people will gossip, hate, slander, and pursue earthly and selfish ambitions and other similar things. This kind of life is below the standards of God. In contrast, the eagle lives high up in the mountains. Likewise, an eagle Christian lives at a high spiritual altitude in God.

Chapter Two

The Prophet Habakkuk uses a deer instead of the eagle to illustrate the high spiritual altitude of an eagle or spiritual Christian.

Habakkuk 3:19 says, *"The sovereign Lord is my strength; He makes my feet like the feet of a deer, He enables me to go on the heights."*

In Habakkuk chapter one, the prophet was in a spiritual valley. He was at a very low spiritual altitude; at a ground dove level. The spiritual and moral decadence of the nation of Judah had perplexed him almost to the point of despair. In his depressed, discouraged, and perplexed state of mind, he complained to God. However, in chapter two he went into his prayer tower to pray and God gave him a life-changing word to take him to a high spiritual altitude. God said to him in Habakkuk 2:4 that, *"The righteous will live by his faith."*

This revelatory word caused him to change his perspective of the situations he was facing. In chapter 3:2 of this same book, he begins by praying for revival. He prays,

"Lord I have heard of your fame; I stand in awe of your deeds, Oh Lord renew them in our day, in our time make them known; in wrath remember mercy." By verse 17, he confesses that he was going to serve God no matter what. He closes the book in verse 19 by comparing his feet, that is, his upward spiritual mobility in God, with that of a mountain deer that lives on the mountain.

You will notice that both in Habakkuk 3:19, using the deer to illustrate high spiritual altitude and Isaiah 40:30-31, using the eagle for the same purpose, God is the one who gives the strength through faith to gain altitude.

I mentioned earlier that the eagle comes down to get food, protects its territory, and helps its fellow eagles in molting periods. What is this molting period? First, there is the annual molting period when eagles systematically change their feathers by nature. When this is happening, it does not affect the eagle's ability to fly. However, there is a different kind of molting period. This occurs in the mid-life of an eagle. It is said that at this period of an eagle's life it experiences chemical changes in its body, resulting in unusual negative behavioral changes.

During this molting period, it becomes secluded. At this time, the eagle finds a lonely place in a valley and stays there alone with its head down. It is unable to shed tears because its tear ducts have stopped producing tears. Its feathers fall out. It stops searching for food, and its talons (feet) become fragile from constant efforts to find insects in the ground to eat. The eagle loses its weight, energy, motivation, the ability to fight, and to soar. It is at the lowest ebb in altitude. Without help at this stage from other eagles, it is hopeless; death is imminent. At this point, other concerned eagles, especially those that have been through similar experiences, fly over this molting eagle, making sounds to alert it that they are there to help. They help the molting eagle by dropping food close by so it may eat and be strengthened and prepare to soar again when it is renewed. This is the time that other eagles should leave their high altitude geographically to rescue a fellow eagle.

In similar manner, an eagle-like Christian is required by God to come down in a ministerial way, while maintaining their own high spiritual altitude to rescue other Christians who are defeated or have fallen. Paul exhorts the Galatians in chapter 6:1-2 that when a fellow Christian is down spiritually, *"You who are spiritual should restore him gently. But watch yourself or you also may be tempted. Carry each other's burden and in this way you will fulfill the law of Christ."* The law of Christ is love.

Eagle-like Christians also are required by God to minister to sinners of various kinds in their low conditions, in order to save them, but still possess the eagle's mountain top mentality. In humbling ourselves in this way, we are seeking to lift up those who are morally and spiritually low.

The Apostle Paul is a model of lowering oneself in order to identify with them and subsequently lifting them up, as is stated in 1 Corinthians 9:19-22. He says, *"Though I am free and belong to no man, I make myself a slave to everyone, to win as many as possible. To the Jews I became like a Jew, to win the Jews. To those under the law I became like one under the law (Though I myself am not under the law), so as to win those under the law. To those not having the law I became like one not having the law (Though I am not free from God's law but I am under Christ's law), so as to win those not having the law. To the weak I became weak, to win the weak. I have become all things to all men so that by all means I might save some."*

We should be like the Apostle Paul who could adapt to all kinds of conditions, situations and people, while still maintaining his high moral and spiritual altitude in Christ.

God's assignment for the church is to transform society and not for society to transform it. Some people boast in the

Chapter Two

fact that they have spent many years living and working among the poor and the oppressed, but they have never sought to transform them into morally and spiritually victorious people. If I so choose to live my life with the morally and spiritually depraved, but do not influence them to change for the better, my work will ultimately be in vain. My pursuit should be to do everything to change them. God has called us to be agents of change. There is nothing to boast about, if we have not helped people to change their conditions. We should be like eagles for God. Eagles come down to help a molting eagle soar again not to live there with them. This is what God has called us to do when we come down to minister to others. Are you doing this?

Chapter Three

THE GOLDEN EAGLE FLIES FASTER THAN OTHER BIRDS

The second amazing characteristic of the Golden Eagle is that it flies faster than other birds. The eagle has powerful wings and flops them at slower intervals than other birds, yet it flies much faster than them all. It can fly as fast as two hundred miles per hour. Normally, it flies at about one hundred and twenty miles per hour.

What causes it to fly so quickly? The eagle has what is called primary feathers, which are shaped like human fingers. As a result, air passes through the tips of the feathers on its wings, so causing the eagle to soar. Air moves faster at the top of its wings than at the bottom, which causes a drag. Normally, this drag should cause the eagle to slow down. Instead, the opening of the primary feathers results in the formation of small whirlpools that make it possible for the eagle, without much effort, to use the current of the wind to increase its flying speed. Other birds are not designed this way.

In like manner, a Christian is designed by God to be able to open his/her spirit to the power of the Holy Spirit and depend on God to cause him/her to soar without humanistic efforts. Depending on humanistic efforts to serve God only lead us to frustration, desperation and defeat, as is recorded in Romans 7:15-25.

There is a marked difference between an eagle and an immature Christian, as it relates to air passing faster through the top of the primary feathers and slower at the bottom. The non-spiritual or immature Christian is slowed down by his or her lower sinful nature. This is because the Holy Spirit does not move freely and quickly through the natural desires and habits of the carnal human nature. As a result, the upper nature of the regenerated human spirit experiences a drag that is caused by the opposing response of the lower human nature. Galatians 5:17 states the problem very clearly. It says, *"The sinful nature desires what is contrary to the Spirit, and the Spirit what is contrary to the sinful nature. They are in conflict with each other so that you do not do what you want."* The regenerated human spirit is in harmony with the Holy Spirit, so the sinful human nature is opposed to both. Romans 7:15-25 relates the same truth about this conflict.

The differences between the upper nature and the lower nature produce a drag effect and more. They also cause a tug-of-war effect and, therefore, prevent the immature Christian from soaring spiritually. This is so because the spirit of such a Christian is not opened to the flow of the Holy Spirit as it should. Therefore, the opposition of the sinful nature impedes his or her spirit from carrying the lower nature freely upward, when the regenerated spirit wants to soar spiritually.

In contrast, the spiritual Christian, whose spirit is open to the flow of the Holy Spirit, overpowers the opposing drag of the lower nature and takes it quickly upward, as it soars in Christ. Romans 8:2 summarize this truth beautifully. It says, *"…Through Christ Jesus the law of the Spirit of life set me free from the law of sin and death."* Galatians 5:16 reinforces

Romans 8:2. It says the law of sin and death is the active negative principle that is pulling the immature Christian down, like the law of gravity. The law of the Spirit of life is the Holy-Spirit-implanted principle in the regenerated spirit of the Christian that pulls upward like the law of aerodynamics.

As I stated earlier, the air develops at the top of the primary feathers of the eagle small whirlpools that cause it to soar freely without being impeded by the slower movement of air at the bottom of these feathers. Likewise, the Holy Spirit produces whirlpools of spiritual anointing that prevent the lower nature of spiritual Christians from pulling them down when they want to soar. This is a great truth that Christians need to learn and apply, if they want to experience upward spiritual mobility in Christ.

Let us relax in God by faith and allow the current of the Holy Spirit to enable us to soar into the heavenly realms, where Christ wants us to be spiritually.

Chapter Four

THE GOLDEN EAGLE HAS BRILLIANT EYESIGHT

The third amazing characteristic of the Golden Eagle is this: It has brilliant eyesight. It can survey an area of about four and a half square miles from a mountain. Also, it can accurately identify its prey two hundred feet away and is able to attack it coming from this same distance without missing its target.

The eagle has an exceptional God-given ability to see. It has double vision in each eye, while a human being has one. The reason for this double vision is that the eagle has two foveae (sockets) in each eye that have a number of small cones (sensory elements in the retinas of its eyes) tightly grouped together that cause its vision to be very brilliant.

The eagle's double vision is not the only unique feature of the eagle's sight; it can also see with its eyes closed. This is a result of its two clear eyelids named nictitating membranes. An eagle can close them to protect its eyes from the heat of the sun, the beaks of hungry eaglets that are seeking food or other impending dangers to its eyes and still see.

Every Christian should have double vision. He or she should be able to see things from both a natural and spiritual perspective. The Holy Spirit indwells all Christians so that they might see the things that God has graciously given to them. 1 Corinthians 2:9-10 says, *"...No eye has seen, no ear has heard, no mind has conceived what God has prepared for those who love Him. But God has revealed it to us by His Spirit. The Spirit searches all things, even the deep things of God."*

Christians should also be able to see spiritually even when their physical eyelids are closed. Too many Christians are only able to see things from the natural, humanistic perspective, physically and intellectually. They are enslaved by natural sense perception. Christians should see things

Chapter Four

through the discernment of the spirit. 1 Corinthians 2:12,15 states, *"We have not received the spirit of the world but the Spirit who is from God, that we may understand what God has freely given us"* (Verse 12). *"The spiritual man makes judgments about all things..."* (Verse 15).

As the eagle uses its brilliant eyesight to target its prey or food, so Christians should use their God-given spiritual eyesight to target spiritual food, which is the word of God, and lay hold on it. They should be able also to see their divine purpose and pursue it. The eagle Christian should see what God wants him or her to see, even when he or she is physically asleep, through dreams, visions and revelations. There are many examples of these in the Bible. Peter, in Acts 10, and Paul, in Acts 9, are examples of Christians seeing visions and revelations while their physical eyes were closed.

In order for a Christian to see far and deep spiritually, he or she must mature spiritually. The Apostle Paul bemoans, in 1 Corinthians 3:1-3, that the Corinthian Christians were not seeing spiritually, because they were not growing spiritually. In Hebrews 5:11-14, the writer has a similar concern, because when they were supposed to be teachers they needed elementary teachings about Christianity again. The Apostle Peter also emphasizes the importance of spiritual growth, in order to see at a distance and in depth spiritually. 2 Peter 1:5-

8 says, *"For this very reason, make every effort to add to your faith goodness; and to goodness, knowledge; and to knowledge, self-control; and to self-control, perseverance; and to perseverance, godliness; and to godliness, brotherly kindness; and to brotherly kindness, love. For if you possess these qualities in increasing measures, they will keep you from being ineffective and unproductive in your knowledge of our Lord Jesus Christ."* However, note carefully the warning in verse 9 of this chapter as follows: *"But if anyone does not have them, he is nearsighted and blind, and has forgotten that he has been cleansed from his past sins."* Eagle Christians are seeing Christians. They have brilliant, spiritual eyesight, which can see reality and truth with their eyes closed physically.

We must also see in our spirit the glory of God and change into what we see. 2 Corinthians 3:18 says, *"We all, with open face beholding as in a glass the glory of the Lord, are changed into the same image from glory to glory, even as by the Spirit of the Lord"* (KJV). We must also see the purpose that God has called us to fulfill, generally and individually. In Ephesians 1:18, Paul prays for Christians to know the hope of their calling. When we see our purpose, we will be gripped by it and endeavor to fulfill it, as Paul points out in Philippians 3:14, in support of this. This verse says, *"I press on toward the goal to win the prize for which God has called me heavenward in Christ Jesus."*

Chapter Four

Another thing we need to see is the incomparable resurrection power of Christ that is in us, which must be released by faith through the anointing of the Holy Spirit, Ephesians 1:19.

When we see these things spiritually, our faith will not be in man, or any other creature, but in the power of God, as is stated in 1 Corinthians 2:4-5.

Chapter Five

THE GOLDEN EAGLE FEEDS MOSTLY ON LIVING THINGS

The fourth characteristic of the Golden Eagle is that it lives mostly on living things such as: fish, rabbits and birds, to name a few. It resorts to eating dead carcasses usually only when it cannot find the foods it desires. Usually, the Golden Eagle is different from many other species of eagles and scavengers, like crows, that strive on dead meats.

Based on what is stated above, there is a great lesson here to learn, as Christians, regarding the eagle's diet. We should feed on living food, which is the word of God. Jesus says in Matthew 4:4 that man should live *"on every word that comes from the mouth of God."* Jesus also says in John 6:63, *"The words I have spoken to you are spirit and they are life."* This implies that the human mind and spirit should live on the word of God, which is living food and living truth that comes directly from God through inspired persons and angels.

Any word, idea, teaching, doctrine, concept, philosophy, and belief that is not in harmony with the word of God that is revealed in the Bible, is not spirit, life, nor truth. Therefore, it is not living food. It is dead food that pollutes both mind and spirit. If you feed on it, it will destroy you rather than nourish you.

Some persons, in their search for mental and spiritual food, have ended up in the wrong places with the wrong companions craving for their food, like the prodigal son in the parable in Luke 15:15-16. Some of the foods they are feeding on are cult teachings, witchcraft and occult teachings, horoscopes, false philosophies, false ideologies, false scientific theories, and false doctrines in church; all that which deny and reject the Lordship of Jesus, salvation by faith through Christ alone, holy living according to the word of God and the Bible as the inspired word of God. Dead foods include focusing on bad memories and evil imaginations. These are dead foods that destroy the mind and spirit of those who feed on them.

Even some Christian seminaries, Bible colleges, universities and other institutions of learning, have been feeding their students on dead foods. One example was given by the famous theologian and philosopher, Dr. Francis Schaeffer in his book, the complete works of Francis Schaeffer. He tells the story of a prominent Episcopal Bishop in America who confessed, close to the end of his life, that when he was a young man seeking for spiritual and intellectual bread, he went to a prominent seminary in search of bread but came out with his mouth full of pebbles. This is one of the worse indictments against a Christian institution I have ever heard. Other examples of dead foods are gossips, slander, ungodly music, movies, books, magazines; and so on that Christians and other people are destroying their minds and spirits with.

In contrast, the Apostle Paul says, in Philippians 4:8 that, *"Whatever is true, whatever is noble, whatever is right, whatever is pure, whatever is lovely, whatever is admirable - if anything is excellent or praise worthy - think about such things."* This is, indeed, a wide categorization of the essence of living food; feed on them. He also says in Romans 12:2 *"Do not conform any longer to the pattern of this world but be transformed by the renewing of your mind. Then you will be able to test and approve what God's will is - his good pleasing and perfect will."* When we think on these things, we will be renewed and transformed by living food. In Greek, the original language in which the Book of Romans was written, the word *"renew"* means to renovate. So when we feed on the living word it renovates our minds. The result of this is the transformation of our spirit into the likeness of God, as verse 2 of Romans 12 indicates. The word *"transform"* in Greek is the equivalent of metamorphosis in English, which means change of character and form, among other things. So the living word, which is living food, radically changes those who feed on it.

The origin of the contrast between living and dead foods began when Adam and Eve rejected the truth of God and accepted the lie of the devil in Genesis 3. Their decision to eat dead food, which is the lie of the devil, instead of the food of God, polluted them and plunged them and the entire human race and nature at large into death and moral and spiritual entropy or decay (Romans 8:19-22). This was the result because Adam was the representative head of the human race. The choice of lie over truth will continue to be practiced by the majority of mankind until the end of time, according

Chapter Five

to biblical prophecies. Romans 1:21-32 gives a theological synopsis of the choice of Adam and his descendants. In 2 Thessalonians 2:9-12, the disastrous climax of choosing dead food over living food is predicted. God will abandon them to the inevitable consequences of their choice. It says, *"The coming of the lawless one will be in accordance with the work of satan displayed in all kinds of counterfeit miracles, sign and wonders, and in every sort of evil that deceive those who are perishing. They perish because they refuse to believe the truth and so be saved. For this reason, God sends them a powerful delusion so that they will believe the lie and so that all will be condemned who have not believed the truth but have delighted in wickedness."* So anyone who chooses to eat dead food instead of living food is not like the Golden Eagle.

There is another very important lesson to learn from the eating practice of the eagle. The eagle does not, as a rule, catch a prey that is too heavy for it to carry. But, if it does, it is in serious danger because the weight of its prey will pull it down on land or in water, which will expose its life to danger. Once its talons and beak grips its prey, it cannot easily release them. Therefore, the eagle has to discern what it can carry, even when it is 200 feet away. This means the eagle has to have a high level of discernment. Eaglets are taught by their parents quite early to develop in this area.

Like the eagle, a Christian ought to judge, even from a far distance, what teachings he or she can bear and absorb. I observed with dismay a number of young Christians, especially those who are educated, influential, popular and powerful, who think the moment they become Christians that they are able to function like mature Christians. They want to be teachers and leaders in high positions, even before they learn the elementary teachings of the Bible. Many of them have become causalities in the church because of this ignorance and stupidity.

Paul was an Apostle of great wisdom who dealt with this matter with great skill in teaching the Corinthians, as is recorded in   1 Corinthians 3:2. He stated, *"I gave you milk, not solid food, for you were not yet ready for it. Indeed, you are still not ready."* This is why every immature Christian needs a pastor and other mature Christian leaders to teach, train, coach, mentor, disciple and guide them. God has given to the church apostles, prophets, evangelists, pastors, and teachers to prepare and lead Christians to maturity (Ephesians 4:11). These leaders are ordained by God *"to keep watch over"* the souls of Christians, as Hebrew 13:17 tells us. There are many Christians who are very unsettled. As a result, they move from church to church, meeting to meeting, and conference to conference; having no consistent pastoral leadership and are not accountable to anyone. These Christians are usually unbalanced, confused, immature, and self-conceited. They usually see themselves as right and super-spiritual, yet have no spiritual depth. Some of them have been severely damaged by food (teaching) that they could not bear. Let me give you one example.

Early in my pastoral ministry, I had a colleague who regarded himself as an evangelist. He never had a pastor or a home church that he was accountable to. He visited various churches and sometimes preached. There was a group of young Calvinistic intellectuals who were pushing Calvinistic theologies, especially predestination, election and reprobation. They were conducting lectures and discussions in the city where my colleague lived so he attended for a period of time. The discussions and the teachings were too heavy for him intellectually, spiritually, and emotionally. He was so disturbed, confused, and perplexed that he became literally sick and emotionally depressed for a period of time. Another minister and I had to minister to him before he was restored to a state of wellness. This is a warning to those who are following in the same vain.

So, from this you can see that there is food in a distance that God has for us, which we need to identify and be accurate like the eagle and not miss it. We should be able to target what God has for us but many times we do not. What has happened on several occasions is that satan set up counterfeit food in the same direction where God's food is and it usually looks more attractive to the human sense perception than God's. This is why some immature Christians have missed God's living truth but have ended up with the devil's lie. You can avoid that if you experience what Hebrews 5:14 and Romans 12:2 say respectively. Hebrew 5:14 says, *"Solid food is for the mature, who by constant use have trained themselves to distinguish good from evil,"* while Romans 12:2 exhorts, *"Be transformed by the renewing of your mind. Then you will be able to test and approve what God's will is - his good, pleasing and perfect will."* This is how we accept truth and overcome error.

In the Bible, there are truths that are close to you and there are some that are far. You should be able to discern from afar, go for it, and get it. Are you?

Chapter Six

FOUR ENEMIES OF THE GOLDEN EAGLE

The Golden Eagle, like other eagles, has a number of enemies that threaten its well-being and its very life but the Golden Eagle is a very wise creature it can skillfully deal with them most of the time.

The first enemy I will focus on is the snake. This creature climbs up the rocky mountain and heads for the eagle's nest in the rock. It is a particular danger to the eagle's eggs and eaglets. It is a definite danger to the next generation of eagles. However, the male eagle, which is always alert, usually  vehemently defends its nest. Eagle Christians are always alert to the dangers the devil poses that are depicted by the serpent in the Bible and defeat him. I will expound on it more in chapter 7 and 12, which deals with the eagle and family life.

The second enemy or potential enemy is the wind of a storm or hurricane. Storms and hurricanes are threats to most birds and animals. Whenever they sense them coming, they seek to find a place of safety or fly as fast as they can to get away, but never can.

However, the eagle does not fly from nor oppose them. In contrast, if the eagle is in its nest when it senses a storm or a hurricane coming, it goes to the edge of the rock, flies out into the storm, and uses the wind force of the storm to soar higher. You would have noticed that the eagle does not fly away from nor fight a storm or hurricane; it uses it to its own advantage.

How does the eagle use the wind of a storm or hurricane? As is stated in chapter three, the eagle has primary feathers, which part at the top like human fingers, that allow wind to pass through them quickly and thus aids its soaring ability. These same feathers help to give it stability in the midst of a storm or hurricane. What the eagle does is to close its wings a little towards its body; by so doing it reduces the wind capacity and, therefore, relaxes itself in it. It only moves the tip of its primary feathers to make adjustments when the wind speed changes. As a result, the wind causes the eagle to soar higher with minimum effort.

In a similar way spiritually, an eagle-like Christian uses the storms and hurricanes of life, which are the problems, trials, and sufferings that he or she experiences, to soar to higher levels in Christ. He or she does not fight nor run from these negative experiences but capitalizes on them.

Eagle Christians know that God works all things for their good, according to Romans 8:28. They also know and believe that God is with them so they can relax in the midst of the worse experiences. They accept the fact that they are more than conquerors through Christ (Romans 8:35-39).

The third enemy of the eagle is the trapper. The trapper is one who seeks to desensitize and deceive the eagle and then catches it in his net. There are stories of trappers who study the movement, activities, likes, dislikes, and other characteristics of the eagle in order to trap it.

For example, they will daily set freshly caught fish in nets in the area where the eagle frequently searches for food. They attach cords to the nets and dress themselves in clothes that resemble the area that they are in and hide themselves there.

They repeat this activity for days. At first the eagle observes the fish with suspicion and stays at a distance.

However, as it visits the area each day, observes the fish, and senses no impending danger, it is gradually desensitized and goes closer and closer to the net. Then it finally decides to go into it. The trapper immediately pulls the cord and closes the net. The more it tries to get out, the more it is entangled in the net; it is hopeless unless someone comes to rescue it.

This is a perfect example of how the devil desensitizes many Christians over a period of time and catches them in his deceptive nets through various means. For example, the devil uses enticements such as worldly pleasures, power, fame, romantic relationships, and even ministries that God did not call them to do, as means to trap Christians. In doing so, he entraps them, knowingly and unknowingly, to do his will rather than God's will.

The Bible exhorts us in 1 Thessalonians 5:21 to *"test everything. Hold on to the good."* Every Christian has a responsibility to examine carefully and prayerfully everything at all times so that he or she might not be desensitized and be caught in the traps of the devil.

Chapter Six

The fourth enemy of the eagle we will scrutinize is the raven. The eagle is regarded as the raven's greatest enemy. The raven is also one of the deadliest enemies of the eagle. It has been observed that when the eagle is flying around and taking it easy the raven descends onto its back and plucks out some of its feathers. This is a major problem for the eagle.

The Raven's Impending Attack On The Eagle

Since the Golden Eagle feeds mostly on living things, it is unable to catch living creatures when some of his feathers are unsystematically taken out. This is so because when feathers are taken out contrary to how God has designed it to be there is a whistling sound when the eagle is flying, which scares away its prey.

When the eagle is in this problem, what does it do to resolve it? It flies back to the rock on the mountain, which is its favorite habitat, for its restoration process. It is said that when the eagle goes back to the mountain it hides itself in the hollow of the rock for approximately forty days. During this period of time, it does a number of things.

First it spreads out its wings and beats them on the rock in order to weaken its feathers. Then it proceeds to pick out its approximately 7,200 feathers, which amount to 16% of its total weight. The eagle then waits until new feathers are grown over the approximate forty-day period. While it is waiting for its new feathers to grow, it is sustained by the food that was absorbed just prior to going to the rock.

When the feathers are grown back, the eagle prepares itself thoroughly before it resumes its usual functions. This is usually a daily routine for the eagle before it goes about its activities. It passes all its feathers through its beak, which has a preening gland that produces oil. This activity takes about 2½ hours.

Chapter Six

This process produces the following results: It cleanses, seals, and oils its feathers. The purpose of the sealing and oiling of the feathers are 1) to prevent too much air getting under its feathers; 2) to prevent too much water getting under its feathers during rain; 3) to help it glide faster through the air and 4) to reduce the sound when it flies, so it can capture its prey much easier, without scaring them away.

It should be noted that often times, as soon as the restored and rejuvenated eagle flies from the rock to resume its normal functions, a raven is waiting to carry out a similar attack again. The raven swoops down into the eagle's back with the intent to pluck out some of the new feathers. Because of its short neck, the eagle has a disadvantage in protecting its back.

The raven, like the eagle, is known as a wise bird, calculates the distance of the eagle from above then launches down onto its back. If the raven is allowed to pluck out some of the new feathers, the eagle would have to repeat a similar process like what it has just completed. This would be fatal for the eagle, because it has just completed the process without food and would not be able to remain alive without food much longer. This puts the eagle in a great crisis. How will the eagle solve it?

In order to resolve the problem, the eagle capitalizes on two of its great strengths: wisdom and speed. The eagle knows the limited high that the raven can function conscientiously. When the raven pitches on its back, the eagle immediately ascends with great speed beyond the altitude that a raven can remain conscious, which is said to be normally about 10,000 feet above sea level. In contrast, it is said that the eagle can fly about 40,000 feet above sea level. Therefore, when the eagle carries the raven to that level in a short span of time, the raven goes into a coma. The eagle then slants its body, which causes the raven to fall to the ground and dies. This subject will continue in chapter 7.

Chapter Seven

SPIRITUAL TRUTHS WE SHOULD LEARN FROM THE GOLDEN EAGLE AND ITS ENEMIES

There are a number of parallel truths between the Golden Eagle and the eagle Christian as it relates to enemies. The snake, an enemy of the eagle, quietly and subtlety climbs the rock to the home of the eagle to attack it. The rock, in the Bible and Christian theology, often times symbolizes Christ.

The hymn writer says, *"On Christ the solid rock I stand."* Jesus also says, *"The wise man builds his house on a rock"* (Matthew 7:24). Evidently, this refers to God and His truths. In a spiritual symbolic manner, the snake is symbolic of the devil and his demons going into the presence of God, the Rock, to attack Christians. How could this be? Well, there are many mysterious things concerning what God does and allows that we do not understand and may never understand, but they are true. Let me give you some biblical examples of God allowing satan and a demon to enter His very presence to accomplish God's purposes.

Job 1:6; 2:1 says, *"The angels came to present themselves before the Lord, and satan also came with them."* In 2 Chronicles 18:18-21, the prophet Micaiah says, *"I saw the Lord sitting on His throne with all the host of heaven standing on his right and on His left. And the Lord said, who will entice Ahab King of Israel into attacking Ramoth Gilead and going to his death? One suggested this, and another that. Finally, a spirit came forward, stood before the Lord and said, I will entice him. By what means? The Lord asked. I will go and be a lying spirit in the mouths of all the prophets, he said. You will succeed in enticing him, said the Lord. Go and do it."*

So, it is evident that the devil and his demons are permitted by God to enter His presence to attack His people, as in the case of Job. However, God wants His people to defeat the devil and his demons the way the eagle defeats the snake on the rock. We need to learn this lesson and practice to defeat the devil and his agents in our lives. God permits satan and our enemies to attack us that we might learn to win warfares, soar to higher dimensions in Christ through our victories, and bring honor and glory to Christ.

A similar thing happened among Christ's apostles. In Luke 22:28-32, the prediction of Peter's denial of Christ is stated. Jesus says that satan asked permission to test Peter. Notice, **he asked permission** to enter the very presence of Jesus, who was filled with the Holy Spirit without measure, to test Peter. Jesus gave him permission but prayed for the restoration of Peter. He did not pray to stop the testing nor the denial but for Peter's restoration. The fall and restoration of Peter was intended to help train him to become a mentor and a minister of restoration for other disciples when they fell. What a great lesson to learn. God allows even satan to enter His presence, (like the snake that climbs the rock to attack the eagle) to attack His disciples, so they might be trained to fight warfares and win and help to strengthen others, as a result of their experience. Truly, He works all things for good to them that love Him and are called according to His purpose.

In the case of Judas, in John 13:27, he was with Jesus at the communion table but, ironically, as soon as he ate the bread, satan, the serpent, entered him. We are opened to the attacks of satan and his demons, even in the presence of God, by God's permission. Therefore, we should be alert to the devil's actions against us every moment of our lives. Are you learning from the eagle in this regard?

The second enemy, the wind of a storm or hurricane, refers to a violent force of nature. A storm or hurricane is evidently not a being with senses and reason; they are neuter genders. Many, if not most, of our problems in this world are neuter; even though they are activated by intelligent spirit beings or by natural God-made principles of nature. For example, the storm in the book of Jonah was activated by God to teach Jonah a well-needed lesson. The storm in Luke 8:22-25 seemed to have been satan-activated because it started after Jesus decided to cross the lake and the fact that Jesus rebuked it. The different storms in the Book of Acts seemed to have been natural occurrences of nature through natural principles functioning in a fallen world, Romans 8:19-23. The point is this: There are a lot of events in our lives as Christians and sinners that are experienced from birth until death. Try as we may, we cannot prevent them nor stop them when they are in motion. How should we deal with them? We should respond in a parallel manner to the eagle.

Chapter Seven

As I said earlier, the eagle does not fight the wind of the storm and hurricane. What it does is discern the direction the wind is blowing and instead of fighting it, the eagle positions itself in the direction of the wind, closes its wings slightly, and allows the wind to propel it upward.

Hear me. The circumstances that come into our lives are intended by God to help us soar in spiritual experiences and maturity. They are neuter vehicles preordained by God to help commute us forward and upward. In the case of Jonah, God sent a literal storm to teach him to surrender to God's will. In the life of Paul, God allowed many kinds of sufferings and trials to weaken his naturally strong personality so that he might depend on God, as recorded in 2 Corinthians 12:9-10. Paul says, paradoxically, in verse 10 of this same passage that, *"When I am weak, then I am strong."* This means that the weaker our human nature is through sufferings, the stronger we are spiritually.

It is interesting that the eagle understands the value of the wind of a storm or hurricane and intelligently uses it rather than fighting it. If the eagle fights the wind, it will be hurt or killed. If we constantly fight the circumstances, situations, and conditions that God sends and allows to come our way, they will destroy us.

Another interesting thing is that the eagle only slightly adjusts its primary feathers when the wind changes. When the situations in our lives change, it's an indication from God that we should make adjustments, only to the degree we ought to change. May God help us to learn. The eagle uses the power of the wind and so conserves its strength. This literally means that the wind becomes a blessing to the eagle. Our sufferings and trials are indirect God-sent blessings but often we do not see it this way and so miss the blessings. Paul was an eagle Christian who learned to be content in every situation.

He says in Philippians 4:11-13, *"I know what it is to be in need, and I know what it is to have plenty. I have learned the secret of being content in any and every situation, whether well fed or hungry, whether living in plenty or in want. I can do everything through Him who gives me strength."* Do you relax and let your problems cause you to soar, or do they cause you to fall?

The trapper, the eagle's third enemy, cannot catch the eagle in his net, if he does not desensitize it. We need to realize when we are being desensitized by our enemies. Anytime we begin to feel more relaxed in sin, or become more attracted by it, we are being desensitized. **Run for your life!**

Chapter Seven

Eve ate the fruit because the serpent desensitized her by a lie. Adam did the same because Eve desensitized him by her action. Samson was desensitized by Delilah in Judges 16. As a result, he lost the seal of his covenant with God; he lost his strength; he lost his political position; he lost his reputation; he lost his freedom; he lost his eyes and, finally, he lost his life. What a tragedy!

But notice the contrast to these; Potipher's wife could not desensitize Joseph with sexual enticements and the Babylonians could not desensitize Daniel with food, favor, threats and power, as is seen in the book of Daniel.

The trapper seeks to use all kinds of familiar things that naturally appeal to us in order to trap us. But never let him trap you by desensitizing you. If you examine everything every time through the spirit, you will not be deceived. **Let the trapper wait in vain.**

The eagle's fourth enemy, the raven, can teach us some great parallel spiritual truths that can revolutionize our lives.

- The first enemy, the serpent, enters the very presence of God - by permission - to attack the eagle Christian.
- The second enemy, the wind of the storm or hurricane, represents all the negative neuter

experiences of life. When God allows them to come into our lives, we should use them to soar to higher spiritual levels, while using minimum human efforts. They are God-allowed means to be used to help us soar higher.

- The third enemy, the trapper, uses things that we love or are attracted by to entice us. But we should be alert at all times.

- The fourth enemy, the raven, attacks the eagle in its back from above, but the eagle has the solution. I will proceed to show you.

Satan is called the prince of the power of the air. His demons operate in that realm with him. In Daniel 10, we see one of satan's powerful ravens called the Prince of Persia, who was controlling the atmospheric realm of the Persian empire. However, Daniel, a spiritual Golden Eagle, was able to soar in prayer to God on the first day of his prayer and fasting, although the actual result did not arrive until the 21st day.

John was exiled on the small island named Patmos, because he was a spiritual eagle, as is written in the book of Revelation. In Revelation 1:10, John was suffering persecution, but he was in the spirit. In Revelation 4:1-2,

John's eagle status became even more evident. He says, *"After this I looked, and there before me was a door standing open in heaven. And the voice I had first heard speaking to me like a trumpet said, 'come up here, and I will show you what must take place after this.' At once I was in the spirit, and there before me was a throne in heaven with someone sitting on it."* After he heard the voice and received the call to soar like an eagle, he ascended in the spirit up to the throne of God. What an eagle!

Paul had a similar eagle-like experience, as is recorded in 2 Corinthians 12:4, when he soared to the third heaven or paradise and saw things that he was not permitted to share, not even with other Christians. What an eagle trip that was!

However, despite these great experiences, the devil and his demons were waiting to swoop down onto his back spiritually, like the raven does to the eagle. Paul had a low experience at Troas, 2 Corinthians 2:12. He had no peace of mind. Although God opened a door for ministry, he left. But praise God he went to the Rock, Christ Jesus, because in verse 14 he praises God for causing him to triumph in Christ, despite his experiences.

Elijah is another case. He had many mountain top experiences but he ran from Jezebel in 1 Kings 18-19. In

Numbers 20, God told Moses to speak to the Rock, Jesus Christ, (1 Corinthians 10:4) but Moses left the presence of God and struck the rock instead of speaking to it.

When John the Baptist, (the forerunner of Christ, who baptized Him, introduced Him as Messiah to the world, and inducted Him into ministry) was put in prison, he began to doubt who Christ was, (Matthew 11). Nevertheless, Jesus regarded him as the greatest Old Testament Saint that was ever born.

All these men knew what it was to be on the spiritual Rock and to soar. Yet the raven, satan's agent, flew onto their backs and plucked out some feathers and they were temporarily incapacitated. Paul left Troas, Elijah wanted to die, Moses disobeyed God by striking the rock, and John the Baptist doubted who Jesus was.

However, all of them went to God, the Rock, and flew back into service, except John who died for God. David says in Psalm 23:3 that, *"He restores my soul."* This is a process we must all go through over and over until we finish our earthly journey.

Another important point about the raven is that it attacks the eagle's back from above. This is parallel to the fact that we Christians are fighting against principalities and powers in high places, Ephesians 6:12. Note carefully, the similarity of the raven attacking the eagle's back with the facts about the armor in Ephesians 6:10-18. The armor does not have any covering for the back. The back is vulnerable.

There are two main ways to protect the back of an eagle and a Christian. The first one is not to expose the back to the enemy. The second is to let someone else protect it. The eagle is not able to protect its back but other eagles can and will do so if they are present. It is when the eagle is alone that the raven attacks its back. The parallel truth for a Christians is this: Do not be a lone ranger Christian, Hebrews 10:24-25. However, there are times when one cannot avoid being alone. God ordained it to be so. In those times, remember to soar as fast as you can to the Rock, Christ Jesus, who is high above principalities and powers, Ephesians 1:20-23. Remember also that positionally every Christian is seated in heavenly places in Christ, Ephesians 2:7 and Colossians 3:3. Therefore, the position of a Christian is far above the same principalities and powers. We need to know and believe this to exercise our authority and powers over our spiritual ravens.

The soaring Christian is one who goes beyond theoretical truths to experience forward and upward progress in Christ. Nothing or no one can defeat such a Christian, because he or she is more than a conqueror in Christ, Romans 8:35-39. Do you believe this? Let these truths be riveted deeply into your conscious and sub-conscious mind like the Psalmist in Psalm 119:11 says, *"Thy word have I hid in my heart that I might not sin against you."*

It will revolutionize your life from inside out.

Chapter Eight

THE GOLDEN EAGLE AND FAMILY LIFE:
A BIBLICAL OVERVIEW

Before I address specifically the analogies of the Golden Eagle and family life, let me highlight some general and biblical facts about family life.

It is evident to even the simplest of persons that family life is in a serious crisis. The fact is that it has been in crisis since the first sin entered the world in Genesis 2. When Adam and Eve were made by God, as recorded in Genesis 1 and 2, the world was a place of bliss. There was no conflict in the relationship of this prototype couple.

God made the man with a need for a female wife, not a same sex wife, so he created a woman out of the essence of the man's body by using one of his ribs. God made and gave to him the woman suitable to be his wife. Someone has interpreted the term *"Helpmeet"* in the King James Version or *"Helper"* in the New International Version as *"Companion of his likeness."* I concur with this view.

This couple was the bedrock of the family. Subsequently, the family became the obvious bedrock of a community and, by extension, the world. They were in harmony mentally, spiritually, physically, emotionally and socially. This is obvious from even a casual observation of Genesis 1 and 2. The man, Adam, confessed this delight when he received her. In Genesis 2:23 he exulted, *"This is now bone of my bones and flesh of my flesh; she shall be called woman, for she was taken out of man."*

This is the minutest unit of family life and of all social structures in every society, like the nucleus of an atom is the minutest part of matter. As the nucleus of an atom contains great power and the splitting of it releases devastating power, so marriage, the smallest unit of the social structure of a society, contains great power. When split, its releases devastating power on the entire society. God, the Creator, knowing the power of marriages to make and break the world, gave one of the earliest and most important commandments to mankind. In Genesis 2:24, it reads, *"For this reason shall a man leave his father and mother and be united to his wife, and they will become one flesh."*

In this statement, God reveals three fundamental and universal principles that marriage, the family and, subsequently, the world at large is dependent on to succeed God's way. The consistent violation of these principles has contributed to all the sociological problems in the world, directly or indirectly, since the home is the habitat that produces every citizen of the world.

The three fundamental and universal principles are these: leave, cleave, and become one flesh. Notice the mandate: First of all, it is the man who is commanded to leave, unite with his wife, and become one flesh with her.

My own experience in dealing with marriage problems and my observation and research have shown that sons leaving their mothers, especially, and uniting with their wives have been a problem for many husbands to fulfill, but not so with wives generally. However, the one flesh element is more a problem for wives than husbands, because while men generally are more interested in the physical aspect of sex, women generally are more interested in the relationship aspect.

Paul says in Ephesians 5:21-33 that the love of a husband for his wife and the respect of a wife for her husband are prerequisites to fulfill these principles. However, there is a more fundamental principle that must be kept, if husband and wife are going to fulfill these three fundamental and universal principles that underline a successful marriage. It is this: husband and wife must not break one truth in order to obey another. This is also true in every area of life. Every truth of God should be obeyed. This means that the truths of God that are commanded should be synergized in our lives for us to fully please God and be successful in marriage and all other areas of our lives. I will proceed to explain what is meant by this.

Notice that marital problems began when Adam broke one of God's laws to fulfill another. God said the man should *"Unite with his wife,"* but God also commanded Adam in Genesis 2:16-17 that, *"You are free to eat of any tree in the garden; but you must not eat from the tree of knowledge of good and evil, for when you eat of it you will surely die."* Take note of the warning, if you eat of it, *"You will surely die."* He

Chapter Eight

was commanded not to eat of the forbidden tree and he also was commanded to unite to his wife. His wife was deceived by the satan-possessed serpent, so she broke the law of God. Adam united with his wife in breaking the law of God. He obeyed one but broke the other.

Notice again this fundamental truth: Do not break any of God's laws to fulfill another except where God clearly permits it, as in the case of breaking a law to fulfill an oath in the Old Testament.

The devil tried the same trick with Jesus in Luke 4:9-11 and Matthew 4:6-7. If you are the son of God, he said, throw yourself down. For it is written: *"He will command his angels concerning you, and they will lift you up in their hands, so that you will not strike your foot against a stone."* Jesus answered him; *"It is also written: do not put the Lord your God to the test."* Satan was trying to get Jesus to use one part of the Bible to break another part.

Remember that God is truth, John 13:6; 16:13 and the devil is the father of lies, John 8:44. Truth or lies is at the foundation or root of every action. God is at the root of every truthful act and the devil is at the root of every untruthful act. This means that every action is either inspired by a lie or a truth.

Family life crises began because Adam and Eve believed the devil's lie rather than God's truth, (Genesis 3). The moment that Adam ate the forbidden fruit every area of his life entered into the realm of death, which is based on lies. Before Adam sinned, he and Eve were united, but the moment he sinned a five-fold family crisis started. First, the marriage was spiritually disconnected from God because they died spiritually. Second, the marriage was theologically disconnected from God, because it was controlled by satan's lie. Third, the marriage was emotionally disconnected from God and each other. They were afraid of God and Adam blamed God for giving him Eve. Fourth, the marriage was socially disconnected, because Adam blamed Eve for the problem. And fifth, the marriage was in the process of death and was not permanent anymore, because death would eventually separate them.

Here is an important observation: Before Adam and Eve sinned, there was no mention of God authorizing Adam to rule over Eve or Eve to rule over Adam. Pay special attention to this: God only commanded Adam and Eve to rule over other creatures and subdue the earth, Genesis 1:28. It is evident that Adam was the legal head of the human race according to Genesis 2; Romans 5:12-21 and 1 Corinthians 15:21-22. However, despite this fact, God did not give him a specific command to rule over Eve until they sinned. When

Chapter Eight

Eve sinned, she unofficially assumed the leadership over Adam by influencing him to disobey God, Genesis 3. At that point, God took a decisive step to establish a law authorizing Adam to legally rule over Eve, Genesis 3:16. It says *"Your desire will be for your husband and he will rule over you."*

Therefore, before sin entered the world there was no law authorizing a human being to rule over another. God was their leader and would have remained their leader directly, if they had obeyed Him perfectly. This is how it will be when the fullness of God's kingdom is come at the end of the age.

As a result of man's fall, God has instituted various categories of leaders in the world to prevent the wickedness of man from bringing total chaos to the world at large. It is within this context that marriage is so pivotal to the well-being of society. Where the family goes, there goes the world, because it is in the home that the human character is fashioned.

The problem of the original family increased in the second generation when God rejected the worship of Cain and Cain murdered Abel. It continued to increase in a later generation, as is manifested through the polygamous practice of Lamach, a descendant of Cain. He was the first to marry two wives, contrary to God's command in Genesis 2:24. A few hundred years later the world was so corrupted through the evils of Adam's descendants that God had to destroy the world, except for four families, married couples.

Again I say, where marriages go, the communities go and, subsequently, nations and the entire world. Marriages are in a severe crisis today and divorce and remarriage are occurring in large numbers

Since the state of marriage is such, we need to learn some lessons from the family life of a Golden Eagle couple as follows in chapter 9.

Chapter Nine

THE GOLDEN EAGLE AND FAMILY LIFE:
COURTSHIP AND MARRIAGE, PART 1

If marriage is to be restored to the original intent of God, the process of courtship will have to improve drastically between male and female. The process of courtship today is far from what it should be despite all the books, videos, lectures and other educational mediums on the subject. It is usually frivolous, superficial, too casual, impure, fun-focused and the like; for the most part it is a joke.

If courtship is to improve significantly in depth and quality there is a lot we can learn from the female Golden Eagle, especially women. Some women are so desperate to be in a relationship or to get married that they are ready to accept those who first propose to them. This is foolish and dangerous, because courtship helps to determine the quality and duration of marriage. One marriage counselor and researcher concluded that of the marriages he has researched 5% are happy, 10% are fair and the other 85% just merely exist. This is a sad story.

Even the marriages of Pentecostal and other evangelical Christians, who promote doctrinally and theoretically Bible-centered and God-focused marriages, are in a serious crisis, according to recent reports. George Barna, one of America's leading church researchers, has found that approximately 40% of evangelical marriages are ending in divorce, virtually the same trend as the secular world.

Look with me at the courtship pattern of Golden Eagles. An eaglet leaves its parents' nest at about one year old. From then until about five years old it will fly, hunt for prey/food

Chapter Nine

and then seeks to find a mate. How the process of courtship is conducted is very instructive and should put many women, even Christian women, including very educated and experienced ones to shame.

Both Christian and secular researchers agree that the Golden Eagle and other eagles are monogamous. That is, they mate with the same partner for life, as a rule. At four or five years old, a male eagle searches to find a female spouse. At this period, its innate instinct drives him to search for a mate, but its outcome is not going to be as simple as that. The male eagle is going to be put to severe tests to prove his qualification for a wife.

It is said that the male eagle goes out scouting to find a partner. He tags a female and follows her around for days. When the female eagle realizes this, she goes for a flying stroll, about ten thousand feet high and goes around in circles for days with the male following her patiently. If the male still has hope of marrying her, which he usually does, he follows her closely for as long as is required. Then the female goes down to earth, picks up a branch that she can carry up to high altitude, eight to ten thousand feet above sea level, while the male follows closely behind her, as he is tested. She drops the branch suddenly and, if he wants to pursue her in marriage, he must catch it before it touches the ground. If he does, it shows his skill at the first level of testing. So he passes this exam successfully and tries to return the branch to the female but she shows him no attention. Whether he is embarrassed or not, he must continue to follow her, if he wants to marry her. In continuing her series of tests, she goes down and picks up another branch heaver than the first, flies faster and lower, says most researchers, then drops it. The male must catch it again and tries to give it to her, but she ignores him again. If at any time he fails her test, the courtship is over immediately and she chases him away. She is putting him through a series of acid tests to see if he is potentially a good husband and father. This is important to her, because after marriage he will have to catch their eaglets when they fall from their nests at the cliff of the rock at high altitude.

Oh that woman would take men through serious tests like the female eagle before they even engage them, much more marry them.

These tests continue until the female comes down to the ground, picks up a piece of log about her body weight, approximately fifteen pounds, and flies about five hundred feet above sea level, drops it suddenly, and the male eagle must once again catch it before it falls to the ground, before

Chapter Nine

courtship can continue. If he does, there is one more test before the marriage ceremony can take place at high altitude.

The testing methods of the female Golden Eagle are systematic. It moves from the lower to the higher level. Take note that before the final test she requires that he catches a log that is approximately her body weight.

It is significant that up until this point there is no physical contact between them. This is a very important lesson to take note of. First it shows that the female eagle has standards, values and expectations that the male eagle respects and is willing to wait until the process is completed before he touches her and gets her in marriage.

After the male eagle passes the tests of the female eagle that I have mentioned above, there is one final test before the marriage takes place. The female eagle flies to high altitude with the male eagle, who is still interested in marrying her, in hot pursuit. When she reaches the height that she has chosen to fly, she closes her wings, it is said, and begins to fall towards the ground. At this stage, the male eagle must pass his final test by catching her. He has to pass the previous test that requires him to catch the log about the weight of her body before she would trust him to catch her. This is the first time he is going to touch her. What he does is flies beneath her, catches her, and the female eagle then flips over on his back, and they fly to a rock, lock their talons and wings, while making screaming sounds to each other in the process of the marriage ceremony. From then on, a lifelong marriage begins. However, if he fails to catch her, the courtship is over. It is obvious that both male and female eagles are purpose-driven from before courtship to marriage. Are you? I will continue this subject in chapter 10.

Chapter Ten

THE GOLDEN EAGLE AND FAMILY LIFE: COURTSHIP AND MARRIAGE, PART 2

Let us now observe some valuable lessons that Christians, and even non-Christians, can learn about courtship from the Golden Eagles that qualify or disqualify one for marriage.

First, both the male and female Golden Eagles know instinctively when they are ready for marriage. Notice that at about one year old the eaglet is sent on its own by its parents to fight life for itself. This is a lesson for us parents. There should be a time to send our children on their own to learn about life after we have given them the necessary training and set the required examples. From age one year to about three years, the eagle knows instinctively that it is not yet ready for courtship and marriage. However, at about four to five years it senses the urge to find a life's partner in marriage. Observe that both the male and female eagles have the same urge for courtship simultaneously and that there is never any multiple courtships going on at the same period with other eagles.

The Bible clearly states that God has gifted some people for marriage and others are not. Still there are others who choose not to marry and some are made eunuch by men so they will not get married. This is stated clearly by Jesus and Paul in Matthew 19:11-13; 1 Corinthians 7:7, 17 respectively. Jeremiah, Paul, John the Baptist and Jesus were gifted and called by God to be single. However, these are exceptions to the rule laid down by God in Genesis 2:18 that says, *"It is not good for the man to be alone. I will make a helper suitable for him."* This statement has two evident implications: (1) Man needs another human being and (2) Normally, the man needs a female wife as a normal rule instinctively, like the eagle.

However, while the eagle has instinctive rules to follow, humans have instinctive, rational, social, and divine rules to follow. When they ignore or violate them, the results are social, moral, and spiritual crises and various kinds of other sufferings and problems by chain reaction. In a similar manner as the eagle, there is a time when men and women feel the desire to find a partner or spouse of the opposite gender. Same sex relationships in marriage have no place in God's agenda for marriage. Same sex marriage is a perversion of God's plan for marriage, as a result of satan and man united against God.

In ancient societies, including Africa and Asia, fathers choose partners for their sons and daughters from the time they were children. The children have had no choice. This practice does not fit into the lessons from the eagle. Therefore, this is not the kind of marriage I am addressing. I am dealing with those that require the potential husband and wife to choose.

When a man or woman senses the desire to get married, there are some general rules to follow and for Christians there are even more stringent biblical rules to follow.

First, let us consider some general rational rules to follow. The following are some of the most fundamental qualifications that indicate marriage-ability (one's readiness for marriage).

The first is adaptability. A person who cannot or is unwilling to adapt to change is not ready for marriage. No man or woman is ready for marriage until he or she is willing to adapt to all the necessary changes and demands that marriage will bring; and there will be many. There will be social, economic, mental, emotional and other changes, as the marriage begins and progresses. In order to be adaptable, one has to be flexible. Not in principle, which should be changeless, but in methods and other changeable situations and circumstances that are connected to things such as age, gender, culture and various other challenges. Men and women are different in many ways. So there will be a need for a lot of flexibility in marriage.

The second qualification that one needs before he or she gets married is the ability to solve problems or live through them. One cannot escape problems, even if he or she is single, and it is multiplied after marriage. Therefore, if one is not willing to deal with problem-solving, such a person is not ready for marriage.

The other qualification one needs for marriage is endurance. If one does not have a spirit of patience or endurance, he or she should not get married. One needs a lot of it in marriage, no matter how good the marriage is.

Chapter Ten

The next qualification is empathy, which is putting oneself in the position of another, so to speak, in order to see life from the other person's perspective. This is emphasized by Paul in Romans 12:15, where he says, *"Rejoice with those who rejoice; mourn with those who mourn."* Empathy sees and feels life from the perspective of another person. This is essential for the success of every marriage. We cannot afford to see and experience life from the narrow confines of our personal life only. Until one can synergize with his or her spouse in empathy, the marriage is doomed.

Yet another qualification is the ability to give and receive romantic and general love. One should never marry a person, except he or she feels genuine romantic love for the other. This love is at the core of marriage. So, one needs it for his or her spouse from start to finish. Some persons grew up in a home where there was abuse of various kinds. One such abuse is incest. People who have passed through this abuse often cannot receive nor give romantic love. As a result, they are emotionally cold romantically. Some wives have confessed that their husbands had to give them drugs, alcohol or use force to get them to engage in sexual relationship with them, because of past sexual abuse.

The next qualification is the ability to deal with the general demands of life and family life especially. Premarital counseling is being seen more today as a necessity. Research has shown that people who received and applied premarital counseling to their marriage have had better marriage relationships than those who have not.

For the eagle Christian, there is another qualification that includes and surpasses the rest. It is the will or agenda of God for them, as it relates to marriage. Some have the idea that God does not choose a wife or husband for anyone. For me that argument is full of intellectual and theological flaws. The first reason for this is that choosing a marriage partner is second only to accepting Christ as Savior, if you are gifted by God for marriage, as 1 Corinthians 7:7 indicates. It is evident from scripture that God chooses people for special ministries, 1 Corinthians 12 and 14; Romans 12, and other scriptures. He has chosen people such as, Moses, David, Joseph, Daniel, and others as political leaders. He has also chosen people to do various other ministries. So why would he not choose a spouse for someone? In fact, he chose Sarah for Abraham, Eve for Adam, Mary, Jesus' mother, for Joseph. So why not for any other person? I read one argument that says that if God should choose one's spouse and the marriage fails God would be blamed for it. This is a flawed argument. God has chosen people for other functions and they have failed. Do you blame God? For example, God chose Israel to do a special work but it failed. Should we blame God? God chose King

Chapter Ten

Saul and Jeroboam to lead Israel but they failed. Should we blame God? The answer is clear as the midday sun; certainly not.

God does not come to earth, take a man and woman, and force them to marry against their wills. Like anything else, God has His will for them and He wants them to know and then choose it. He wants the person He has gifted to be married to seek His will regarding the God-ordained person that is best suited for him or her. Then he wants each person to choose the spouse He has ordained for each one then pursue their marriage God's way and succeed.

Since God's ideal is for people to get married, as a general rule; and since one man, one woman is the original and perfect will of God for a marriage; it logically follows that when we are looking for a wife or husband, both the male and female should seek God's guidance to find the right person, rather than having a divided heart focusing on different individuals. At first, one will focus on the crowd to find the one. When he or she finds "*the one*," that should be the end of searching.

How does one find and affirm God's choice for him or her. This is why the lesson from the eagle in courtship is very pertinent and instructive. Notice that it is the male that identifies or tags the female Golden Eagle and she is observant by instinct to his romantic interest. Understand that both are in the season of finding a marriage partner. Nevertheless, despite all the desire of the male and the female eagles to get married, the female eagle is not prepared to accept any proposal from any male eagle until he passes her tests, which are the general tests for male eagles. Be cognizant that the right male eagle is prepared to go through every one of her tests without giving up or pressuring her to change her requirements to marry prematurely. There are two general tests in addition to marriage-ability qualifications I have mentioned, plus your personal tests. They are self-sacrificing love for the woman by the man and genuine respect for the man by the woman as it relates to marriage, Ephesians 5:21-33. This love is not the romantic love we talked about earlier. This is what is called in Greek "*agape.*" Agape is unconditional love. It causes the husband to serve his wife sacrificially. It also inspires the wife to respect her husband no matter what. Therefore, love and respect work together and have a circular and reinforcement effect on each other.

Here is a lesson that non-Christians and Christians women and men need to learn from the eagles. Do not break your principles to get married to anyone. If you do, you will have to continue to do so to keep the marriage. There is a businessmen maxim, which says that whatever you use to get

Chapter Ten

customers, you will have to use to keep them. If you lower your standards to get a woman or a man, you will have to continue doing so to keep him or her.

There is a sad situation in our world and church today, when it comes to courtship and mate selection. It makes no difference if one is rich or poor, educated or uneducated, professional or non-professional, ministers or church members; there is a culture of unprincipled and foolish approach to courtship and mate selection.

The men are in a rush to get too much too soon without passing any test and the women are too quick to give in by breaking their principles, if they have any. Simply put, women are too easy to get. As some say or believe, they are in danger of *"going on the shelf."* That is they are in danger of not getting married. Therefore, they give up their principles to get a husband they will soon lose because they were not qualified to marry them, but they did. I have known and counseled many of these women; some were at their wits end

One date is enough for men to get under the dresses of even some of the highest ranking society women. I have personally spoken to women who told me that they are willing to agree to have sex with men on the simple verbal promise that they will marry them. In many of these cases, after the men have sampled them, they were gone with the intent to sample other women who would lower their standards based on a lying deceptive promise.

Some women, unlike the female eagle, will engage in all forms of sexual activities with their so called potential husbands based on the argument that, *"If you love me, you will give it to me."* What these women of all ranks do not understand is this, if they really love you they will wait. He will not force or deceive you to violate your body and conscience to satisfy their undisciplined instincts.

On the other hand, there are women who have been telling men that if they cannot go to bed with them before marriage they suspect something is wrong with them. Therefore, they cannot take the risk to marry a man who might not be of any sexual use to them after marriage. What is even worse is that some ministers of the gospel believe this lie and even force their potential spouse to prove themselves before they say, "*I do*." This is a disgrace to the name of Christ.

If Christians and others stay clear of sexual contacts during courtship, the female tests the man thoroughly in every way required, and only marries him if he passes every test, the world would be a different place. We would not have had so many divorces, so much broken homes, so much broken and bitter men, women and children. Research has shown that even adults in their midlife are still wounded from the broken marriages and divorces of their parents.

No woman should accept the proposal of a man to marry her until he passes every biblical, general and personal test she believes a husband should pass before she says yes. Some have been foolish enough to believe and acted upon the idea that *"they will change."* So they went ahead and got married. Usually they changed for the worse, because they got what they did not merit. Some men have made the same mistakes and suffer the same consequences.

Men and women who have forced and seduced their potential spouses to violate their principles and consciences have neither loved nor respected them. These marriages are based on infatuation. Appling the female eagle's practice of prolonged testing of the male during courtship will expose this infatuation falsely called love. If a man cannot submit to your testing, let him go. And the same goes for the woman. We men need to respect women, young and old. I have a three-fold philosophy in relating to women. (1) Women beyond my age category, I treat as mothers (2) Women within my age category I treat as sisters and (3) Women and girls below my age category I treat as daughters. I choose one woman in my age category as a wife and all my sexual activity relates to my wife, Jean. Since I treat older women as mothers, women in my age group as sisters, and younger women as daughters, I have no sexual problems with them, in the same way I would not have sexual relationships with my mother, sisters or daughters.

After the male eagle passes all the tests of the female eagles and they unite in marriage at high altitude on the rock, this begins a brand new phase for their lives.

Some couples have nothing new to give each other on their so called honeymoon night, because they have given away everything already. Therefore, the wedding and honeymoon are just legal formalities that have been spoiled too soon.

Sex is ordained by God as a romantic act that unites the body, emotion, mind and spirit of a man and woman in marriage for life. However, many have turned it into mere fun, commercial business, and all kinds of other purposes. God has three basic reason for marriage: to perpetuate the human race, mutual pleasure between husband and wife in marriage, and to illustrate the mystic union between Christ and His church, Genesis 2:24; 1 Corinthians 6:18-20; Ephesians 5:21-23; 1 Corinthians 7:5-7, and the book of Song of Solomon. However, man has turned it into idolatry and all kinds of evil.

Psychologists, psychiatrists and marriage counselors have discovered that when women are too anxious to get married or to have male relationships, they give away too much too soon and they are used, abused and refused. Heed the command of Philippians 4:6 *"Do not be anxious about anything, but in everything, by prayer and petition, with thanksgiving, present your request to God."*

Marriage should be a life-long relationship. From a biblical viewpoint, divorce is not a part of God's ideal plan for marriage. Divorce is a conspiracy between man and the devil against God's purpose. Therefore, marriage should not be entered into quickly, lightly, frivolously and unprepared. Let your emotions be calm, your mind be alert and balanced, and your heart in tune with the spirit of God. Keep your head tightly screwed on during courtship and marriage.

It is said that *"Love is blind."* But let me remind or inform you that wisdom is not blind. This is why love needs the eyes of wisdom in the choice of a wife or husband. When love and wisdom are united, a person will have the right balance. Love has the right heart. Wisdom has the right mind. It takes God, love and wisdom to choose the right spouse and these are what so many persons in and out of the church do not have. You can have them if your heart and mind are tuned in with God.

Let me close this chapter by saying, if a person applies for a job, he or she has to past the tests. They also need recommendations and must have suitable track records. Marriage is more important than a job. Why should you require less? You should require more.

We have seen that the eagle courts at high altitude. Earlier in the book, in chapters 2 and 3, I told you that the Golden Eagle lives and soars at high altitude. Now the future of the married Golden Eagle couple is destined to be lived at high altitude until death parts them.

When marriage is lived at high spiritual altitude in God, divorce is not an option. It is when couples lives at low spiritual and moral altitude that their marriages run into trouble and end in separation and divorce. Jesus gives one fundament root cause for a marriage that ends in divorce, in Matthew 19:8. In response to his disciples' questions about the lawfulness of divorce and the reason why Moses permitted it, he responded, *"Moses permitted you to divorce your wives because your hearts were hard. But it was not so from the beginning."* A hard heart is a callous heart; a hard heart is an impenitent heart; a hard heart is an unloving heart; a hard heart is an unforgiving heart; a hard heart is an immoral heart, and a hard heart is an ungodly and unspiritual heart. Is there any surprise if it leads to divorce?

Therefore, if you select your spouse, court and live the marriage life God's way, you will succeed.

Soar Like an Eagle 👑 Reign Like a King

Chapter Eleven

THE GOLDEN EAGLE AND FAMILY LIFE:
BUILDING A HOME

This brings me to the Golden Eagles' home after marriage. As important as the courtship tests are, living the marriage life is even more important and difficult. Starting something correctly and successfully and continuing to live it successfully to the end are two different challenges.

Let us focus now on the eagle's nest, which is its home, its main habitat. After the eagles get married, they have to choose a location to build their nest. Remember, that after they left the respective homes of their parents, they spend their time mostly flying and hunting prey. They were on their own. Now that they are married they need a place to lay her eggs and hatch them. This will begin the next generation of eagles from their linage. It will not be only their home but the throne from which they will reign over a specific domain. I will deal specifically with their domain in chapter 13.

The book of Job and Jeremiah give us some insight regarding where eagles build their nest, their home, and their throne. Job 39:27-28 says, *"Does the eagle soar at your command and build his nest on high? He dwells on a cliff and stays there at night; a rocky crag is his stronghold."* Bird watchers and researchers have observed that the bald eagle, as well as other species of eagles, live and build their nests usually in the highest trees However, the Golden Eagle, as a rule. builds it nest on the highest mountain cliffs.

They build their homes at high altitudes because it is advantageous to the individual eagle, the couple, and its future eaglets.   Job 39:29 tells us some reasons why the eagle's nest is built so high. It says, *"From there he seeks out his food; his eyes detect it from afar."* Two things are highlighted: (1) it seeks its food, which is its prey, from there and (2) it does not only seek food from there, it can detect it far and wide. As I said before in chapter four, it can survey an area of about four and a half square miles from the mountain top. From the same height, it can detect its enemies trespassing in its domain and go against them. So it is a place of protection. It also conserves its strength when it flies downward, while increasing its speed to about two hundred miles per hour at times. From this same location, it discerns the direction of the wind of the storm or hurricane and uses it to soar higher with minimum effort. The young eaglets are taught to fly from there also. Therefore, the height of the Golden Eagles' nest is very strategic in a number of ways.

There are lessons to be learned from the eagle's nest. (1) When the eagles get married, they start their own home. They do not live with their parents or anyone else. This is in line with Genesis 2:24, which says, *"A man will leave his father and mother and be united with his wife."* The word united, which is translated *"cleave"* in the King James Version, means to glue in heart, mind, emotion and purpose. I have counseled couples in premarital counseling sessions and also married couples not to live with parents or in any other person's home, except in a temporary crisis situation when wisdom and practical realities demand it. A couple cannot be what they ought to be living under the authority of another family. Some have ignored or rejected my advice and lived to see the negative results and have regretted their decision.

The eagle's nest is built on a rock using wood it finds on the ground not on the rock. The woods that are used to build the foundation of the nest on the rock are larger than the ones that are added to build the structure of the nest. It is built with other materials like prickles, leaves, vines, cotton, and the like. They continue to add to it year after year, until its size reaches as much as ten feet wide and 20 feet high and weighs up to two tons.

Symbolically, a Christ-like home is based on Christ the Rock, who is its foundation. However, the home itself is built with the materials of human character and personalities. Proverbs 24:3-4 says, *"By wisdom a house is built, and through understanding it is established; through knowledge its rooms are filled with rare and beautiful treasures."* A home, then, should be built on Christ with the beautiful Christ-like characteristics of the human personality such as wisdom, knowledge, understanding, love, truth, trust, kindness, faithfulness, righteousness and characteristics of similar qualities. We have to keep on adding to our homes the Christ-like qualities taught in the Bible until death.

Other lessons to be learned from the eagle's nest are as follow: The home should be a place of high spiritual altitude in Christ. It should be a place to produce the next generation. The home is where the members of our churches, students of

Chapter Eleven

our schools, colleges, universities, the workers of the workplace, the members of gangs on our streets, inmates in prisons, and the people from every other area of life come from.

We need spiritual high altitude homes to produce better people, provide more protection, and everything else we need to build a better world. What kind of home is yours?

Chapter Twelve

THE GOLDEN EAGLE AND FAMILY LIFE: CHILD REARING

After the newly-wedded eagles build their home, they begin to procreate. First, the female lays approximately three eggs and sits on them until they are hatched in about forty-five days. Usually, the male eagle will bring food to the female eagle during this period. The male may take turns in sitting on the eggs but not usually. The roles of these married eagles show their cooperation and unity in producing eaglets.

After the parent eagles have built their home, and the female eagle has produced two or three eggs, or after the eggs are incubated, the snake, one of the eagle's most deadly enemies, becomes the greatest threat to the next generation of eagles. As I discussed in chapters six and seven, it subtlety climbs up the side of the rock on the high mountain with the intent either to eat the eggs or the eaglets. However, it will discover that its mission will not be easy; most often than not, it will be thwarted primarily by the male eagle, the undisputed guardian of his home and family. There are times when the mother eagle is the one that defends the eggs and eaglets.

The male eagle and the female also, ferociously attack the snake with their talons, wings, and beaks to kill or expel it from their domain. If the snake is allowed to eat the eggs or the eaglets, it would destroy the next generation.

This is what satan, the spiritual snake, has been doing to sinners and Christians today. Here are ways he has been doing so. He is the author of the abortion culture that kills millions of unborn humans each year. He is the author of the laws that restrict parents from using the rod to discipline children. Satan is the author of all the cartoons and other shows and literatures that destroy the minds of children. Satan is the author of the theory of evolution that leave our

Chapter Twelve

children in no man's land, not knowing who they are, where they came from, how they came, why they exist, and where they go from this planet.

Satan has entered the eagle's nests of many of us Christians also and has been eating the eggs and the children, which are the next generation.

Unlike the male eagle that fights, defeats and chases away the serpent from his home, some of our husbands and fathers are unable to attack the snakes in their homes. They are spiritually impotent. May God have mercy on us and our children.

Many of our young men and women in gangs, authoritarian cult groups, and other such groups, are there because they are looking for authentic male leadership. They are seeking an authentic masculine image. They are bombarded by the female image at home, school and church, while too many men are at wrong places, such as rum bars, gambling dens, drugs houses, and the like.

Some years ago at a church I pastored, we were looking for a teacher for our high teen Sunday school class. A female teacher was suggested. The girls in the class threatened not to attend, if a female teacher was chosen. According to them, they were tired of being taught by women at home, school and church.

We need spiritual male eagles to defend the next generation at home, school, church and elsewhere. Will they come forward?

The next spiritual activity the parent eagles accomplish for their children, the eaglets, is to train them. About three months after incubation, the female eagle starts to teach the young eaglets to fly. Here is what happens: About three months after the birth of the eaglets, she perches over the nest and flops her wings to attack and entice them to fly. At first, they are reluctant to respond. In order to get them to leave the nest and try to fly, the mother eagle tears off the top layer of cotton, and or other soft materials, thus exposing the sticking prickles underneath. This makes the eaglets uncomfortable, for they are experiencing these sticking prickles for the first time. As a result, they respond to their mother's enticement to fly.

When they respond by stretching out their wings, their mother stretches out her wings for them to go on her back. She then flies out at high altitude and suddenly dispatches them from her back. They are now in great danger. They must try to fly or descend rapidly to the earth. Even though they try to fly, they are not yet ready to fly on the first day of practice. Mother eagle, who understands the process of flying, swoops below them and catches them on her wings, which could be seven feet wide when they are opened, and flies back with them to the nest on the rock. This process is repeated until they learn to fly and finally leave home permanently at about one year old. Here are some lessons to learn from a Golden Eagle couple, which will change family life.

Parents should provide a healthy, safe and educational environment for their children. They should teach and train them to go out to start their own lives and homes. There are too many homeless and uncared for children in our society. There are too many of them in unhealthy and abusive homes, where there are mothers and fathers. There are too many who leave home for the wider world with no idea of what to expect; totally unprepared to face life on their own. We, as parents and guardians, need to do better than this. We need to learn from the eagles.

The next lesson we need to learn is that fathers should care for their children like male eagles. In Exodus 19:4-6, God gives Israel some great truths, which apply to all His children throughout time. He says, through Moses in this text, *"I carried you on eagle's wings and brought you to myself. Now if you obey me fully and keep my covenant, then out of all nations you will be for me a kingdom of Priests."* This is profound. When we are too inexperienced and too weak to fly, God Himself, spiritually speaking, carries us like eagles on the wings of the Holy Spirit. The objectives are that we might be a *"Kingdom of Priests."* Kingdom implies a domain ruled by a king, who is Christ. Priests imply a temple where there is a high priest and other ministering priests. Christ is the Great High Priest and we, His children, are the kingdom of priests, whether we are male or female; Jews or Gentiles; slaves or free; rich or poor; black or white; educated or uneducated; whoever or whatever we are, if we trust in Christ, He carries us on His wings so we might become kings and priests for Him. Therefore, we should care for our children like kings and priests. Are you?

Chapter Thirteen

THE GOLDEN EAGLE IS KING OVER ITS DOMAIN

The Golden Eagle is regarded as king among birds and king of its territory. When a married Golden Eagle couple choose to build their nest, as was stated before, they choose a strategic spot at high altitude in the cliff of the rock. From that vantage point, it can survey a wide area from afar. The eagle's strategic position, its speed, its strength, its brilliant eye sight, its ability to soar fast and high, its ability to fight, and its desire and ability to control a wide territory, make the Golden Eagle couple a dominant pair over its chosen domain.

It has been observed that different pairs of Golden Eagles have dominated different sizes of land space, ranging from 10 to 60 square miles. The respective couple will attack other birds, such as the raven, hawks, other eagles, and various animals that trespass into its domain and defeat, kill or chase them away.

The Bible speaks of the kingly and awesome nature and ability of the Golden Eagle. In Jeremiah 49:22, it says, *"Look! An eagle will soar and swoop down, spreading its wings over Bozrah. In that day the hearts of Edom's warriors will be like the heart of a woman in labor."* This is a figurative description of a nation, led by a king, which will invade Bozrah to wage war. The eagle is used pictorially to describe the king that will invade and attack Bozrah. The implication is, from God's perspective, that the eagle is a kingly and war-like bird.

The messages we need to learn as Christians is that just like the eagle is kingly and war-like in protecting its territory, spiritually we should be the same individually and collectively. We should wage spiritual warfare to protect our people, territories and the things that God has entrusted to us.

Chapter Thirteen

In Ephesians 1:19-23 and Colossians 1:28; 2:9, it is stated clearly that Christ is the head over both the church and all principalities and powers. He is also the Creator and Sustainer of everything in the universe.

We, who are united with Christ, by faith through the Holy Spirit, are heirs of God and joint heirs with Christ. Romans 8:17; Galatians 4:7; and 1 Corinthians 3:21-22 affirm that all things are ours. However, to appropriate what is ours, we must know it by revelation knowledge (1 Corinthians 2:9-16 and Ephesians 1:18-23) and exercise faith in the word of God. The righteous live by faith (Habakkuk 2:4 and Romans 1:16). In fact, this is the teaching of the entire Bible, as Hebrews 11 illustrates.

In spite of the fact that we are kings and own all things, Hebrews 2 tells us that we cannot fully appropriate all things now. However, we can possess all that God wants each of us to have. To do so, we must reign as kings like the Golden Eagle. To reign, we must fight, defeat and chase away the principalities and powers or whoever or whatever else that intrudes or trespasses on our territory, Ephesians 6:10-18 and 2 Corinthians 10:4-5. To accomplish this, we must clothe ourselves with the full armor of God and fight in the spirit and with prayer until our lives are ended in this life. We should *"occupy until He comes"* (Luke 19:13 KJV). This means we should rule over our domain for Christ until we die individually or the rapture of the church collectively.

Peter tells us in 1 Peter 2:5,9 that we are a kingly priesthood and John affirms in Revelation 5:10 that Christ has made all Christians *"A kingdom of priests to serve God."* What a lofty position we have! This is why Paul can say in Ephesians 2:6 that *"God raised us up with Christ and seated us with Him in the heavenly realms in Christ Jesus."* Certainly, if we are Christians, we can soar like an eagle and reign like a king; we can and we should. This is why Jesus prayed, *"Your Kingdom come your will be done on earth as it is in heaven"* (Matthew 6:10). His holy angels do His will in heaven. Eagle Christians do His will on earth, and reign over their God-given territories like eagles. Are you an eagle Christian? If you are not, are you going to be?

Conclusion

This book began based on the proposition, at the end of Chapter One, *"That a Christian should live like an eagle."* I used the next twelve chapters to argue adequately why a Christian should do so.

These chapters show that the Golden Eagle lives at a high altitude, soars faster and higher than other birds, has brilliant eyesight, feeds mostly on living things, conquers its enemies, has a model family life and reigns like a king over its domain. These analogies are to teach profound lessons to each Christian, to inspire sinners to become Christians, and to be able to live like the eagle.

As I conclude this book, let me highlight some more important thoughts. God created man in His image and likeness, to manifest God in human form and to have dominion over the other creatures on earth, including nature itself, the entire world, and all that dwell therein (Genesis 1:26-28).

The fact that God created man in His image, and the fact that God is not physical, means that the image of God in man is not physical but spiritual. John 4:24 states categorically that *"God is Spirit."*

Therefore, the essence of man's personality is not flesh but spirit. Man is essentially a spirit-being living in a physical body. Since this is so, we are not a higher form of animals as so many social scientists teach and so many Christians accept. Man is a finite version of God, Psalm 8. Hebrews 2:5-10 gives an interesting exposition of Psalm 8. It tells us that God became like man so that man might become like Him.

However, man's sins have kept him from being like God the way God has designed him to be. Hebrews 2 says that Christ has soared to the highest heaven so that all things are under His feet. However, we Christians, according to verse 9, have not yet soared to the height where everything is under our feet actually like Christ.

Conclusion

This means that everything is not under our control literally yet. However, Christ has gone up ahead of us to bring all Christians to that same height. Hebrews 2:10-11 says Christ died to bring *"Many sons to glory,"* because we belong to *"the same family,"* in order that they will soar and reign together. The more we soar, the more we have all things under our feet and the more control and dominion we have. The more control and dominion we have, the more we reign as kings. In addition to these, the more we soar, the further, wider, deeper and higher we can see spiritually.

Romans 8:29, tells us that Jesus came to restore man to God's original purpose that is stated in Genesis 1:26-28, but restoration has been thwarted in the majority of mankind from Genesis 3 until now.

The purpose of God is to restore man to the image of Christ. This is the ultimate predestined purpose of the birth, life, death, burial, resurrection, ascension, and the coming of the Holy Spirit at Pentecost. The coming of the Holy Spirit is to put into effect, in the lives of Christians, the benefits of the finished work of Christ that He accomplished for them. The Holy Spirit helps Christians to duplicate on earth the priestly and kingly ministries that Christ has been executing at the Father's right hand in heaven. This will continue until the

Second Coming of Christ to establish on earth His everlasting kingdom.

At that time, our lowly bodies, according to Romans 8:23 and Philippians 3:21, will be transformed into the likeness of Christ's resurrected body, so that they may soar at high altitude like the human spirit. What a prospect!

In the meantime, while we wait, Romans 12:1-2 command us to present our bodies, minds and spirits to God so that they might continue the soaring and reigning process until our final transformation.

The above text says *"offer your bodies as living sacrifices, holy and pleasing to God - this is your spiritual act of worship. Do not conform any longer to the pattern of this world, but be transformed by the renewing of your mind. Then you will be able to test and approve what God's will is…"*

The word *"renewing"* in Roman 12:2 means renovating and transformed means to be changed spiritually.

To experience renewal and transformation, we must heed Colossians 3:1-4, which says *"set your hearts on things above, where Christ is seated at the right hand of God. Set your minds on things above, not on earthly things. For you are dead, and*

Conclusion

life is now hidden with Christ in God. When Christ, who is your life appears, then you also will appear with him in glory."

A person who is not born again cannot Soar for he is not an eagle. So repent of your sins and accept Jesus as Savior and Lord and be an eagle. The worldly Christian is like the eaglet in the nest that has not learned to fly. The spiritual Christian is like the adult eagle that has mastered the art of soaring. Which one of these categories are you in? If you are a worldly Christian, leave your spiritual nest and learn to fly. If you are a spiritual Christian continue to soar higher and higher. We will soon soar to our final destination and reign with our Lord Jesus Christ as kings forever. Are you waiting for that day? I am.

About The Author

Revs. Seaton & Jean Wilson

Rev. Seaton D. Wilson is an ordained minister of the Pen-Florida District of the Assemblies of God.

Before transferring his Ministerial Credential in 2007 to the Pen-Florida District, he was a minister of the Assemblies of God in Jamaica for over twenty-five (25) years. Since February 1, 2006 he has been the Senior Pastor of First Assembly of God, Inc., Christiansted, St. Croix, USVI and also ministers on radio and television weekly.

Prior to this he served the Assemblies of God in Jamaica in the following capacities: Lecturer and Academic Dean at the Assemblies of God Bible College 1988 - 2003, and 1991 - 1999 respectively, National Education Director 1994 - 1997, a member of the panel of speakers of its national radio broadcast "Gospel and Song" 1989 - 2005, Pastor of three churches 1980 - 2006 and General Secretary of the entire fellowship 1997 - 2005.

Prior to this, Rev. Wilson was Secretary / Treasurer of the North Trelawny Ministerial Fraternal 1984, Chairman of the United Ministers Association of Manchester, Jamaica 1996 -1998 and Religious Columnist of the Western Mirror Newspaper 1983.

He has been a conference, crusade and seminar speaker in Canada, the United States of America and nineteen (19) Caribbean Islands for the past 25 years.

Rev. Wilson is a graduate of the Jamaica Open Bible Institute 1978 and Luther Rice Seminary 1981 where he earned a Diploma in Bible & Theology and a Bachelor of Ministry Degree respectively. He has been happily married to Jean since 1979 and they have two sons, Joseph and Christoph. His philosophy of life is TO KNOW, BE AND DO THE WILL OF GOD.

ADDITIONAL BOOK BY SEATON D. WILSON

- Reign In Your Domain

CONTACT INFORMATION

Seaton D. Wilson

P O Box 716, Christiansted • St. Croix, USVI 00821

seatondwilson@yahoo.com • 340-277-9094

www.facebook.com/seaton.d.wilson

www.ingramcontent.com/pod-product-compliance
Lightning Source LLC
LaVergne TN
LVHW051135080426
835510LV00018B/2424